King Lion's Den

Table of contents

CHAPTER 1 — 1

Power as a Soulja. — 1

    It could be personal — 1

    It could be financial — 1

    Perception — 2

    Things To Remember When You Feel That The World Is Against You — 3

    So, how do you let God fight your battles? — 5

CHAPTER 2 — 7

Overcoming oneself — 7

    So what does it mean to "overcome oneself"? — 7

CHAPTER 3 — 9

The power of a mug. — 9

CHAPTER 4 — 11

Love — 11

CHAPTER 5 — 13

Analyze — 13

    Dream. — 16

Positive Thinking Will Change Your Life	17
Change Your Thinking	17
The Power Of Positive Knowing	18
Mental health.	19
The Importance Of Originality	20
Talent	21

CHAPTER 1

Power as a Soulja.

Not as a human being. No. play the role in a military. You are not as you are in the war. In the war you are fighting to win. In your role you are attacking your opposition. You are destroying your thoughts of thinking as a functioning being to one that is operating as one in the military. Soldier that is one to defeat everything outside of your spirit that fights against you. Your ammunition, yourself, the tool that God gave to you to manifest.

I'm sure at some point in your life, you've had to endure some form of hardship. We all have.

It could be personal

Maybe you're having trouble with a your spouse or partner, and you just can't seem to get it together. Maybe it's from being complacent for too long and a need for change begins to build inside you. After all, that's what we do right?

We're human. We change. We can get comfortable in our environment, but sometimes we get too comfortable and the desire for change kicks in. It's a good thing, but it can also be your enemy, if you allow it.

It could be financial

Maybe your job doesn't bring in the kind of money you need to do anything more than survive, so when you suffer a setback, you really struggle. You not only struggle with the financial issues, but you also struggle with your emotions. Not having the amount of money you need to live without the fear that comes along with being broke, sucks.

You can be feeling great mentally and physically and able to perform at your best, but if you are struggling financially, there's a good chance you're causing more harm to your body with the stress, worry, and anger that comes along with it. This also plays a role in your personal life as well, doesn't it?

We let our financial frustrations affect ourselves and the personal relationships around us. This brings with it more problems and and suffering, and pretty soon, we're left with only two options.

1. Change

You can change your circumstances to get out of your unwanted situation. It can be difficult to do this, especially when nothing but negativity surrounds you, but if you decide willingly to change your circumstances, you can. It's just a matter of knowing how.

2. Be forced into change

It's human nature to need to be constantly growing, evolving, and changing. If you are stagnant and stick in a routine for too long, what happens? Well, most of the time, you get a feeling of boredom, a desire for change, or despair that comes from being in a stalled state of progression. That's just you telling yourself that you need to change something.

If you were to learn the process a little better, you could really help yourself when it comes to understanding how to endure and overcome the very worst of your life's hardships. Knowing that there is a specific reason you are in a hardship will help you to learn how to get through it in a positive way vs. a negative one.

So what's the process for being able to endure and overcome, you might ask? Well, as you probably already know, no one process will work for everyone, just as there is (usually) no quick-fix solution for the various hardships that come into your life. There are, however, certain ways you can choose to perceive the realities you're hit with.

Perception

Perception is in the eye of the beholder, so if I'm perceiving my life in a negative way, I'm more than likely going to be dealing with all of the emotions and thoughts that come from that perception. In other words, thinking negative thoughts—in any situation—is going to bring out negative emotions. This can get you stuck in a tailspin, and you'll find it very difficult to get past emotions such as anger, sadness, and low self-esteem, which go along with negative perceptions.

This doesn't mean that you shouldn't want to feel those negative emotions—they are a valuable part of progressing and moving forward in your life. The negative emotions are there so you can overcome them. Let's look at just how you can change your feelings of suffering when hardships hit into a new perspective on your life, which will allow you to endure when there is suffering, and overcome when it's time.

The true change happens, when you fully embrace the relationships and connections around you. Manifest through you things that cause construction within yourself, but destruction towards all walls that are against you. Nothing against you can garner victory. Their victory as opposition is your feeding grounds to their destruction. Powerful is the one who eats the opposition as not discouragement but destruction towards the advert forces against thee.

Things To Remember When You Feel That The World Is Against You

1. **This too shall pass.** Everything has an ending – including the bad times and the dark phases. Always remember that it's really not your entire world that is sinking, it's just a point in your life.

2. **You have more control than you think.** You can always find a way to get out of the rut you're in if you truly take the time to control the way you react to things or ask people to help you out. There is always a way.

3. **You never know what tomorrow may bring.** Miracles happen every day and tomorrow is a new day for something better planned for you. Something that may not have crossed your mind.

4. **Some things are going well for you.** Like your health, your friends, or a roof over your head. Remember all the important things we take for granted that we truly can't live without.

5. **You will come out stronger.** You've been there before, you had situations you never thought you will come out of, but you did. We're always tested so we can learn how to stand on our own two feet.

6. **Something good will come out of this.** After the hurricane comes the rainbow. You will either learn an important lesson or you will grow as a person. Look for the silver lining.

7. **Every problem has a solution.** No matter how hard it looks, there will always be a solution for whatever you're going through and in time you will find out exactly how to solve it.

8. **You are not alone.** You are surrounded by people who can help you and a lot of people have gone through the same thing you're going through. Don't believe that you are the only one who is suffering and learn how people got through their difficult times and what they learned from it.

10. **You will feel better if you stop thinking of how bad it is.** Distract yourself. Get your mind off your situation by doing things that make you happy maybe dancing, or yoga or whatever it may be. We all have activities that makes us feel alive.

11. **Being resentful will only harm you.** As difficult as it sounds, you have to forgive yourself and the world if you think it's unfair. It's a long ride full of highs and lows and sometimes you just have to accept it and roll with the punches.

12. **Your pain will make a way for you.** It will either force you to change yourself or change your career or change your life. Pain transforms people and one way or another it will inspire you to do something great; either for yourself or for others.

13. **Some troubles are blessings in disguise.** It might be God's way of leading you to another direction or taking away something that is not right for you. God has a better plan for us. We just have to believe.

14. **Don't ruin your present thinking about the future.** You can be suffering and still appreciate the present. Go out with your friends, travel, try new things, and live your life like you normally would. For one day you will look back on these hard times and feel better about it because you still found ways to enjoy your darkness.

15. **It's all part of your journey.** It's the stepping stone or the road block that helps you get to the next path, or become a better person, or find your calling. Everything happens for a reason. We are meant to go through tough times to see our lives and ourselves in a different light.

By yourself you are closer to God who gives you powers as a source of all strength and clean thinking. God has the garden of life specifically designed for your needs as well as your desires through him because he knows your heart being its creator. What resonances from the power of the heart is at the mercy of spiritual warfare. This fight was never ours. If this fight was ours, we would be in control of the frequencies that come into our soul space.

When you stop and think about it, we are in the middle of several battles. Battles with the weather, our health or that of our family's, our financial situations, relationships with our families and neighbors, and within ourselves. The question that is plaguing me is how to let God fight your battles?

So, how do you let God fight your battles?

Everyone is different and we are all facing battles on various levels. What I'm starting to understand as I research verses for what seems to be A LOT of posts about courage (my constant struggle these days) is that we need to ask and then let God.

Could it be that simple? To simply make our requests known to God and then ALLOW Him to work?

The opposite of how to let God fight your battles would be trying to fight ourselves. I think we should explore this also because we might just recognize ourselves.

So, what does fight your own battles mean? I believe this looks different for everyone, but do any of these sound familiar to you?

- Travel through life with prayer only as an afterthought- you know, the point where you are desperate.
- Pray, but don't leave your situation with God. You continue to worry and fret and problem solve.
- Pray half-heartedly. You know you should pray and leave it with God, but you just can't seem to place your confidence in Him.
- Read multiple books and devotionals trying to convince yourself that God is the solution to all your problems, but don't allow yourself to get to the point where you step out on faith.
- Ask God for help and then try to solve your situation yourself.

I am beginning to understand the importance of placing my situation, my hurts, fears, anxieties, and regrets into God's hands and then letting go. Stepping away. Standing still.

"Clean" energy and "tainted" energy have different vibrations associated with each. Clean energy gives one a sense of direct communication with the most high. A calm spirit of gratitude of things created by God with a space of understanding the afflictions and affirmations the world provides to the harmed and enlightened. As if all things are still, melodic, and meditative. Tainted energy speaks from a place of gloom and despair. A lost of all affirmation of an external environment, one becomes one with a trance state to destruct in the route of self destruction.

CHAPTER 2

Overcoming oneself

The dictionary defines "overcome" as "to get the better of in a struggle or conflict; conquer; defeat: and "to prevail over (opposition, a debility, temptations, etc.)

So what does it mean to "overcome oneself"?

It refers to conquering and defeating that part of you that stops you from setting, striving and achieving your goals; that part of you that stops you from enjoying life and living it to its fullest.

So what is that part of you that would want to stop you or sabotage your success?

First identify what is the emotion that holds you back. Is it fear, bitterness, guilt, resentment, shame, regret, feelings of worthlessness, hopelessness, anger or something else? I have also found, from experience with clients, that a lack of forgiveness is also almost always involved in the equation? Who do you need to forgive? Yourself?

Thus, step two is to release the emotion and that is where the process of forgiveness enters.

Overcoming one's self is one of the greatest gifts one can receive from the universe. Many people spend years, decades, and lifetimes trying to figure out the magic potion to their balance in their existing.

You work incredibly hard balancing your life -- maintaining evenness to be happy from the moment you wake up until you go back to sleep. You're multitasking, which is another word and activity for balance. You strive for: work life balance, a balanced diet and health routine and a balance with family, friends, social life.

It's a moment to moment challenge; juggling, slipping in and out of the events of your daily life to find some, any balance that will give you happy peace... body, mind and spirit. Balance, integration, harmony, stability, equilibrium, steadiness, oneness, symmetry -- We want it! "Want" is the key word here.

What do you want for your life? That's the balance question and it's crucial to find the answer so you can achieve the precious stability you desire. True balance comes from knowing yourself and your purpose in life. It's a lovely, full time job. When you know your purpose, your reason for being, you have a "base for balance" to count on even in the roughest, most demanding times.

But what if true balance is understanding that the chaos of one's self is the order of understanding what needs to be brought into this world from you. Great things can be produced from disarray. Not once have a thinker not doubt his or her ability in sound mind but through the ability of the reflections of life, the interactions and handling of the reflections of life and the result that came brought a creative journey thats unmatched by any other human being on this planet. The taboo and darkness that speaks pain to you and eats the pain of the receptive. Receptive in all ways of what the eyes tell and leed with tears. Receptive as to not only what the mind embraces but the longing of the starving inner man's kept.

It's incredible as I knew I would have to become closer to the spirit one day. Even when I was younger, I carried a wise aura to do things out of what I could manifest from the playgrounds of my mind. There was not a number of quotes I didn't create for those that were aware of my nature to follow.

Creative energy is additive. From the creator and the receptive. The mind is infinite as it was bestowed to us by an infinite deity, God himself. The spiritual fact that we reflect infinite God, Mind, can have a powerful effect on our everyday lives. When we pray to yield to this Mind, acknowledging God's full knowledge of all that is good and true – and that He imparts this knowledge to us as His reflection – we find more and more that we know just what we need to know.

CHAPTER 3

Love

An instrument of peace. Speak of love from the heart that you hold. Genuine love comes from a place where the heart skips a beat. Left not for what's said in the physical but unconditional in all ways that are expressed.

Genuine love is not a love that uses other people or just has people in their life - where they can make a profit from them. Genuine love forgets the self - and is fully present for the other, for the sake of the other. Genuine love gives of its time, effort and energy for the sake of the other, not for the sake of the self. In genuine love, you care for the other for the sake of caring for them. People are present in your life because you care about them and their well-being. Genuine love is patient and understanding; it approaches the other with love. It does not have a usury mentality. It is tender, merciful, and encouraging, even in times when it offers constructive criticism. Genuine love never points back to itself, but always points back to the one who is loved. Genuine love does not just have people in their life for self-promotion, or to better their self-esteem, or for their own self-interest or self-worth. People who genuinely love others have the people that are in their life because they care about them and love them. People who genuinely love each other show it, express it, and cherish it, without expecting something in return. They give of themself merely to give of themself. They do not have ulterior motives. They are genuine and true. They are authentic.

Please do not give falsehood in doings. All of many beings are looking for the truth in human expression as falsehood can be seen a mile away. Love in love. To be of love in love is to be a vessel of thanksgiving and embody the character of it in addition. Not of throwing the term in falsehood from a place of not who is he or she. Keep in mind as a being of heart the oppositions of the spirit. Prepare the spirit to act in ways that are non tarnished. Invincible against all ways that destroys the foundation of self, as the instrument of self is unharmed by the grasp of heavenly abilities preceded by God. When something in common is absent, appreciate the art of each creation. As created by an original God, we are created as original beings in likeness of him.

A journey down the highway of life brings to the fore a bit of creation in all of its glory.

You've heard the saying "Stop and smell the flowers." Yet daily we pass by so many glimpses of God's creation without pausing, even for a moment.

Not only do we miss the chance to smell flowers along the path, but we miss beauty surrounding us.

Are you conscious of the variety of trees, plants, shrubs or flowers along your daily treks? What if we could fully notice the summer's green, the winter's white, and the fall's magnificent paintbrush of colors?

Most of the time I suspect we fail to hear the birds and other wildlife rustling about. And what about feeling the gentle breeze -- God's finest form of air conditioning -- or noticing the brilliance of our own human form?

I love to walk slowly with the awareness of the movement of my own legs and feet.

And at the top of creation, in case you need a reminder, is you. If you want to experience and appreciate God's rich variety in creation, simply look at yourself, your neighbor and every other human being.

As one of the greatest boxers of all time was wont to say: "I'm (You're) the Greatest!" Yes, God made you and saw that you were good.

To appreciate creation might not even require us to go outside. We can look at one another and give thanks for the diversity of our personalities, gifts, talents, characteristics, etc., as manifested throughout the many seasons of our lives. Over the course of a lifetime, we grow in wisdom, age and grace.

CHAPTER 5

Analyze

Analyze to me. Analyze to you. What's really the truth is within you in regards to the likeness of what can be seen. The vessel of the human mind be extended as far as it can be stretched. Smell more than the sensation. But smell that gives account to a recent or distant memory. Talk not just for the sake of communication but talk in the creation of self constructed within you.

Communication - we all think we know what it is. I talk, you listen, you talk, I listen. Pretty simple, right? Well.... maybe not. Most of us have experienced miscommunication on some level. Usually, we are surprised that our message wasn't received the way we intended. From an adult not understanding a toddler telling a story to an employee missing a key task, breaks in communication happen constantly. Often, communication is a result of how our minds work. We simply misinterpret what another person is trying to communicate. Yet, the human mind is geared towards learning language and communication; it is biologically programmed and young children seem to effortlessly learn communication. If communication is such a basic human trait, why does it fail so consistently? See things not only for the physical existence of what's there but through the third eye elongate earth's representation of what's seen as fuel for a creative reality.

Mind is elusive in its existence. Elusive in ways that fleet who thoughts that hold together the pieces of its composition during times of distress.

No matter what your age, several underlying causes can bring about memory problems. Forgetfulness can arise from stress, depression, lack of sleep or other health problems. Other causes include side effects from certain medicines, an unhealthy diet or not having enough fluids in your body.

Be that the energy received. Let not this energy lie in you. Recognize the attack where it is. Analyzing followed by understanding are the grasp of all within reach.

Imagine what you can while you can. Imagine all that you can. Even beyond what you think is your infinity. Your infinity is beyond. The true definition of infinity be true to the limitless God gave you. As there is breath in your body. There is breath in the cycle of what you can create.

How will you know your potential if you never venture to the edge of your limits?

Your comfort zone is a place where you feel secure though it is not where you will discover your potential.

People believe they must venture out of their comfort zone often and I caution them against it. Primarily because you become a thrill seeker if you push your limits without integrating the lessons learned.

Human beings are wired for growth, an essential component to life. You need only interact with those with little growth to see how they perceive life through a narrow filter.

Venturing to the edge of your limits is frightening because it involves stepping into the unknown where you risk failure and defeat, but also compromise your self-esteem.

This is one way of looking at it, what you aim to lose instead of what you have to gain.

Even though terrifying, what you will gain is far more valuable to your personal growth and what you're likely to accomplish.

Even if you fail. Even if you hurt your self-esteem, you will have pushed to the edge of your limits and expanded your possibilities.

It is in losing where you succeed.

You literally fail your way to success, while many people assume success is a series of consecutive wins.

Even the most talented amongst us fail more often than they succeed.

Similarly, it is unnecessary to go right to the edge of your limits from your current position. It requires gradually extending yourself and pushing past your limitations.

Create right what's right to you. Right to you will be right to somebody else. Creating a beautiful right. Right in all ways healing. Right in all ways of mentioning greater human health. No poor condition left after what's written on what's said. What's written is health to those that need the fruits of your thoughts free to accomplish there ever in the composite of within to win.

Don't be afraid of what's to come.

What's to come is a result of what was. What was made the destiny of self. And the destiny of self had to be held by what's there.

Almost everybody worries about what will happen in the future. The prospect of not knowing if something good or bad will happen to you in the near future can produce a lot of fear and anxiety.

Remember that no one can predict the future with 100 percent certainty. Even if the thing that you are afraid of does happen there are circumstances and factors that you can't predict which can be used to your advantage. Remember that we may be 99 percent correct in predicting the future, but all it takes is for that 1 percent to make a world of difference.

Learn to take it one day at a time. Instead of worrying about how you will get through the rest of the week or coming month, try to focus on today. Each day can provide us with different opportunities to learn new things and that includes learning how to deal with your problems. When the time comes, hopefully you will have learned the skills to deal with your situation.

Sometimes, we can get anxious over a task that we will have to perform in the near future. When this happens, visualize yourself doing the task in your mind. Self-visualization is a great way to reduce the fear and stress of a coming situation and increase your self-confidence.

A lot of times, our worrying can make the problem even worse. All the worrying in the world will not change anything. All you can do is to do your best each day, hope for the best, and when something does happen, take it in stride.

If there was nothing there to begin with then there's power in what could be created from non-substance. All substance in the reality of the true events. All substance in the reality of the heart to the heart stands pair to pair of the soul and the mind. All substance in what bleeds from the pen to the paper as the truth in the transfer of energy heals what can't be touched but what can be exhibited as a human being through cathetic expression. Shed tears of the effectsffsc of a world without consideration. All living beings pain or pave beauty with a smile.

Positive thinking doesn't mean that you keep your head in the sand and ignore life's less pleasant situations. Positive thinking just means that you approach unpleasantness in a more positive and productive way. You think the best is going to happen, not the worst.

Positive thinking often starts with self-talk. Self-talk is the endless stream of unspoken thoughts that run through your head. These automatic thoughts can be positive or negative. Some of your self-talk comes from logic and reason. Other self-talk may arise from misconceptions that you create because of lack of information.

If the thoughts that run through your head are mostly negative, your outlook on life is more likely pessimistic. If your thoughts are mostly positive, you're likely an optimist — someone who practices positive thinking.

Dream.

A dream is a fleet of a nightmare. Scare not. Because they are both manifested in the same way. Go to sleep. See the sleep. When one sees the sleep, he or she sees the thoughts of the unconscious. The thoughts of the unconscious will forever be ignored if it is not entertained by the one with the ability.

The basic rule for success is for you to continue to remind yourself that you are where you are, and what you are because of yourself. You are in your current situation because you have decided to be there.

You have made the individual choices and decisions that have gotten you to your current place in life. If you want to go somewhere else or be someone else, it is totally up to you to make the choices and decisions today that will eventually get you there.

And there are no limits.

Positive Thinking Will Change Your Life

Here is another rule: "If you want your life to get better, you have to get better."

This simply means that your outer world will be a reflection of your inner world. If you want your outer world to improve, you must go to work on improving your inner world.

If you want to have better customers and more sales, you must become a better and more personable salesperson. If you want to have better employees, you must become a better manager. If you want to have better children, you must become a better parent. And if you want to have better relationships, you must become a better person.

The great tragedy is that the world is full of people who are trying to change the outside world without going to work on the one thing that they can control, their own thinking!

Change Your Thinking

Here is another rule: "If you change the quality of your thinking, you change the quality of your life."

And since you can change the quality of your thinking almost infinitely, there are no limits on how you can change and improve every part of your life, in any direction you want to go.

There is a lot of talk today about "positive thinking, and I think that positive thinking is very important.

It is much better for you to think positively about yourself and your possibilities than for you to think negatively. But the danger is that positive thinking can quickly turn into positive wishing and hoping. Positive wishing and hoping can turn a person into a very optimistic and happy failure.

Abraham Mallow said that the story of the human race is the story of men and women selling themselves short, and settling for far less than that of which they are capable. Don't let this happen to you.

The Power Of Positive Knowing

What is better than positive thinking is "positive knowing."

This is where you take the steps and do the things that bring you to the point where you absolutely know, with complete certainty, that you can achieve your goals and be the kind of success that it is possible for you to be.

When you reach the point of positive knowing, no matter what happens in the outside world, even if you lose everything you have acquired, you will make it all back again, and more, because you know how to do it in the first place.

I want to share some ideas with you that have been very helpful to me and to many thousands of other highly successful men and women.

These are all ways of thinking and looking at your world that will enable you to become a far more optimistic, confident, and creative individual in everything you do. These are simple, powerful, proven techniques that you can use to throw off your self-imposed limits and begin moving toward the realization of your full potential.

Dream Big, You Have No Limits

The starting point of great success and achievement has always been the same. It is for you to, "dream big dreams."

There is nothing more important, and nothing that works faster than for you to cast off your own limitations and begin dreaming and fantasizing about the wonderful things that you can become and have and do.

A wise man once said, "You must dream big dreams for only big dreams have the power to move the minds of men."

When you begin to dream big dreams, your level of self-esteem and self-confidence will increase immediately. Your self-image improves. You feel more positively about yourself and your ability to deal with whatever happens to you. The reason so many people accomplish so little is that they never allow themselves to let go and just imagine the kind of life that is possible for them.

Keep all unconscious alive and the liveness be the tools to continue to prosper in write. Write all there is to write from the mind. Use the tool for success, as there is no way to lose in continuing to do all there is to do in the ability of extending self to the limit. There is no limit and the limit is only reached after self. Thoughts spread to erase non-functional human afflictions in all ways positive for the love of folk.

Mental health.

Make it about your health. Use the term in the terms and create health for you and only within you. As the author of your own title, give rise to a birth of whatever brings the fruits needed necessary for your daily endurance on earth. Activity may be obscure to those who are not you. But the alright part about it is that you are the original creation. And what more beauty is there not in what's present first and not second. Second has runner's up spirit. First and at the forefront gives one the ability to create whatever there is needed for themselves as footstones of leadership. Original creates the blueprint. Those that follow thereafter works the blueprint on the terms of the creator. Create and reap the harvest of your works for a lifetime through your legacy, a forever birthed.

Let's face it. Following the crowd is easy.

Doing what everyone else is doing doesn't hardly take any effort.

Being the same as the people in the crowd prevents you from sticking out.

You're not ridiculed if you are a cookie cutter person.

That means being true to yourself, your values and originality is tougher than just going with the flow of the crowd.

I realized that my biggest competitor is and always will be myself.

So why should you want to be an original and be unique?

- You are being true to yourself. Not fighting yourself is an ultimate advantage in being true to your originality and uniqueness.
- You will come up with more fresh ideas and new perspectives on old ideas. Basically, your creativity increases.
- Learning to navigate with your differences gives you more confidence and self-esteem.
- People will view you as a person with something interesting to say.
- You are more apt to try things and expand your world thus making you more interesting.
- You will be happier.

The Importance Of Originality

The bottom line on being original boils down to one thing. You were born original with a unique set of characteristics, traits, talents and skills. If you go with the flow of the crowd, you will never be who you were born to be…

You will be a copy. The same old thing as everyone else.

Where's the excitement in being the same old thing as everyone else? Do you just want to be a copy?

Stepping outside the regular boundaries in order to be unique is not always easy.

- People may think you are weird and avoid you.
- It will be harder for people to relate to you, your actions and ideas.
- Most people won't agree with you.
- You may be ridiculed or persecuted.
- You may spend more time alone and thus find yourself lonely more often than others.

Even though there are some big reasons to not be an original and to just follow the crowd, the positives out-weighs the negatives in being original.

Think about it. If you're not going to be you, who will?

No one.

So your uniqueness won't ever be known or add to the value of the environment, community and world.

That's sad.

Actually, that's really a waste.

Talent

Getting out of yourself for God to take control. Or what some refer to as "getting out of their feelings." There's a self that someone is yielding for assistance. The number of talents one has in self is a number blessed by God as he has bestowed all the things that are good. Let not the fruitation of the talents go by being in what's been left for self without use of self. The crusade of God's work is work that requires a voice of sound thoughts minus the he or she that stands as a man or woman of shortcomings. God being an all provider, he will provide one with the roots one needs wrapped in delivery to nourish all that one needs as a man or woman to accomplish.

Talents and gifts differ per individual. The basic reason why you should use your talents and gifts for God is that God endowed you with that talent.

A talent is a gift or special ability to do something, an endowment unique to you.

It is something that makes you stand out from the crowd; different people have different talents based on God's distribution.

Your talent could be something as seemingly simple as motivating and encouraging others through your words, actions and lifestyle. Or it could be in your desire and willingness to readily lend others a helping hand. It may even be a spiritual gift;

We can go on and on, and we may not be able to exhaustively list the various talents that God has given humans.

God has given everyone a talent and there is no one without a talent, though the degree of "talentedness" may vary.

We understand from the bible that talents and gifts are given to us by God. The measure of talents and gifts are unique per person. God expects us to profit with our talents and gifts. There is hardly any human being who doesn't want to profit when they invest. In the same way, our God is a master investor and He expects us to profit with our talents and gifts. God gave everyone talents and gifts.

In the voice of my forever internal monologue. Straight in all ways that only one can provide. Excluding any exterior communication that can be received. The success provided by mental, physical, and financial success. Attributed by the development of you by you for you.

Water enters your body.

Hydrates you. Put you in a position of wellness. Then exits your body once its task in your body is completed. But the positive effects of the water have forever been left with you in that moment of time. Forever a moment of life but a requirement of enduring wellness as you know what you are running off and the force that are supplying the run for the future. Forever in the name of the energy you received as a result of your strength. You are doing it for the improvement of you but through the improvement of you there is a force that bestows the abilities and ways to create greater. Greater in your eyes and greater in the ways of others taking the perspective seen in your thoughts and applying it for their path of endeavors that sit face to face to each other. Rest found in the words displayed to be used in dismay.

Freedom to love.

Without reservation of social norm. But within all of the capacity the heart has to give as a people. Giving from the heart the truth that can be expressed for the sake of restoration for another heart. Vulgar be not of the afflictions of the world on the heart but received from the spirit above a sense of authentic and genuine healing. Be received love that tells a tale of the truth within that embodies the thoughts and what gives life to another individual. Love be by definition of received in the restoration of the positive for elevation in the fruits of the individual. Love wrapped in a way that unveils and left completely uncovered in its sake for its effect of rejuvenation. Getting out of yourself for God to take control. Or what some refer to as "getting out of their feelings." There's a self that someone is yielding for assistance. The number of talents one has in self is a number blessed by God as he has bestowed all the things that are good. Let not the fruitation of the talents go by being in what's been left for self without use of self. The crusade of God's work is work that requires a voice of sound thoughts minus the he or she that stands as a man or woman of shortcomings. God being an all provider, he will provide one with the roots one needs wrapped in delivery to nourish all that one needs as a man or woman to accomplish.

Leverage as the balance of who you are needs to be created from what you have. What you have in your provide is a keen sense of unity of all things that are broken apart in your soul to create a reinvented image of self. Self that prospers off the shards that were seen and the creation of the new image that is as the old thoughts and existing of what was has come together to create a new, whole idea. Take this new idea and manifest in all that one can to restore the broken pieces of another creation broken at the hands of the demolition of the afflictions of the world. Afflictions of the broken turned into a unit of unity through the togetherness of affirmations.

www.ingramcontent.com/pod-product-compliance
Lightning Source LLC
Chambersburg PA
CBHW082337300426
44109CB00045B/2472